The Wealth Navigator

Mastering Personal Finance in the Digital Era

Maxwell Sterling

Table of contents

Introduction

Navigating the Financial Landscape in the Digital Age

In today's digital age, the financial landscape is rapidly evolving, presenting both challenges and opportunities for individuals and businesses alike. The advent of technology and the internet has revolutionized the way we manage and interact with our finances. From online banking and digital payments to cryptocurrency and robo-advisors, the digital age has transformed traditional financial practices.

This transformation has brought about increased convenience, efficiency, and accessibility to financial services. With just a few clicks or taps, we can now transfer funds, pay bills, and invest our money from the comfort of our homes. Additionally, the rise of fintech companies has introduced innovative solutions that cater to the changing needs and preferences of consumers.

However, navigating the financial landscape in the digital age also requires a heightened awareness of potential risks and challenges. As technology advances, so do the methods used by cybercriminals to exploit vulnerabilities and steal sensitive financial information. Protecting our digital identities, securing online transactions, and staying informed about the latest security measures are essential in this new era.

Moreover, the digital age has expanded the range of financial options available to us. Cryptocurrencies such as Bitcoin and Ethereum have gained popularity, offering decentralized and alternative forms of currency. Understanding the intricacies of these digital assets and their potential implications on the global economy is crucial for individuals and businesses looking to explore these opportunities.

Furthermore, the rise of automation and artificial intelligence has given birth to robo-advisors and algorithmic trading systems. These technologies offer personalized investment recommendations and execute trades at incredible speeds. However, it is important to strike a balance between automated solutions and human expertise to make informed financial decisions.

In this era of constant innovation, financial literacy becomes even more essential. Understanding concepts like budgeting, debt management, and investment strategies is crucial for individuals to achieve financial well-being. Additionally, staying informed about new financial products, regulations, and industry trends can help individuals and businesses adapt to the ever-changing landscape.

IIn conclusion, the digital age has revolutionized the financial landscape, providing unprecedented convenience and opportunities. However, it also requires us to be vigilant and proactive in managing the associated risks. By embracing technology, staying informed, and developing financial literacy, we can navigate the financial landscape in the digital age with confidence and make the most of the available opportunities.

Part 1
Building a Strong Financial Foundation

Chapter 1

Money Mindset

Shifting Perspectives for Financial Success.

Exploring your relationship with money

Money is a fundamental aspect of our lives, influencing our choices, opportunities, and overall well-being. People have different relationships with money, which can be shaped by various factors such as upbringing, personal values, cultural influences, and life experiences.

Some individuals may view money as a means to achieve financial security and independence.

They prioritize saving, budgeting, and investing to build wealth and attain long-term goals. Others may have a more relaxed approach, viewing money as a tool to enjoy the present moment and fulfill immediate desires and experiences.

For some, money can be a source of stress and anxiety, particularly when faced with financial challenges such as debt, unemployment, or unexpected expenses. Such individuals may feel a sense of insecurity or powerlessness when it comes to managing their finances.

It is important to develop a healthy relationship with money that aligns with your values and goals. This can involve setting financial objectives, creating a budget, managing debt responsibly, and establishing saving and investment habits. Seeking financial education, consulting with professionals, and surrounding yourself with a supportive network can also contribute to improving your relationship with money.

Remember, money is a tool that can enable you to achieve your goals and live a fulfilling life. However, it's essential to maintain a balanced perspective and not let money become the sole measure of success or happiness. Prioritizing your overall well-being, including your physical and mental health, relationships, and personal growth, is equally important in shaping a healthy relationship with money.

Cultivating a positive money mindset

Cultivating a positive money mindset is crucial for establishing a healthy and empowering relationship with money. It involves shifting your perspective and attitudes towards money, allowing you to make sound financial decisions and achieve your financial goals. Here are some key steps to help you cultivate a positive money mindset:

1. Awareness and Mindfulness: Start by becoming aware of your current beliefs and attitudes towards money. Notice any negative or limiting thoughts you may have, such as "Money is the root of all evil" or "I'll never be able to save enough." Practice mindfulness by observing these thoughts without judgment and understanding that they can be changed.

2. Challenge Limiting Beliefs: Identify any negative beliefs you hold about money and challenge them. Ask yourself if these beliefs are based on facts or if they are simply ingrained assumptions. Replace limiting beliefs with positive affirmations and statements that align with your financial goals and values.

3. Focus on Abundance: Shift your mindset from scarcity to abundance. Instead of dwelling on what you lack, focus on what you have and the opportunities that exist. Develop gratitude for the money you do have and the financial resources available to you. Believe that there is enough money in the world for you to achieve your goals.

4. Set Clear Financial Goals: Establish specific, measurable, achievable, relevant, and time-bound (SMART) financial goals. Having a clear vision of what you want to achieve with your money helps you stay focused and motivated. Break down your goals into smaller milestones and celebrate your progress along the way.

5. Educate Yourself: Increase your financial literacy by learning about personal finance, investing, and money management. The more knowledge you have, the more empowered and confident you will feel in making financial decisions. Seek out reputable resources, attend workshops, or consider working with a financial advisor to expand your financial knowledge.

6. Practice Gratitude and Generosity: Cultivate a mindset of gratitude for the money you earn and the opportunities it provides. Express gratitude for the financial abundance in your life, whether big or small. Additionally, incorporate acts of generosity into your financial practices. Giving back to others and contributing to causes you care about can foster a positive and abundant mindset.

7. Surround Yourself with Positive Influences: Surround yourself with people who have a positive money mindset. Engage in discussions about personal finance with friends, family, or mentors who have healthy attitudes towards money. Avoid negativity or conversations that perpetuate financial stress or scarcity thinking.

8. Focus on Personal Growth: Recognize that your relationship with money is interconnected with your personal growth. Take steps to improve your overall well-being, including your physical and mental health, relationships, and personal development. Enhancing these areas of your life can positively impact your financial mindset.

Remember that cultivating a positive money mindset is an ongoing process. It requires self-reflection, patience, and consistent effort. By adopting a positive and empowering perspective towards money, you can create a healthier relationship with finances and achieve financial well-being.

Overcoming common financial obstacles

Overcoming common financial obstacles is crucial for achieving financial stability and success. Here are some strategies to help you tackle and overcome these obstacles:

1. Debt Management: If you're burdened with debt, develop a plan to manage and pay it off. Start by creating a budget to track your income and expenses, and identify areas where you can cut back on spending to allocate more funds towards debt repayment. Consider strategies such as the debt snowball method (paying off the smallest debts first) or the debt avalanche method (paying off debts with the highest interest rates first). Explore options like debt consolidation or negotiation with creditors to lower interest rates or create more manageable repayment plans.

2. Building an Emergency Fund: Unexpected expenses can derail your financial progress. Establish an emergency fund by setting aside a portion of your income each month. Aim to save three to six months' worth of living expenses to provide a buffer in case of emergencies. Start small if necessary, and gradually increase your savings over time. Having an emergency fund can prevent you from relying on credit cards or loans during challenging times.

3. Budgeting and Financial Planning: Creating a budget is a fundamental step in managing your finances effectively. Track your income and expenses to understand where your money is going and identify areas where you can cut back or optimize spending. Set financial goals and create a plan to achieve them. Consider working with a financial advisor or using personal finance apps to help you streamline your budgeting and financial planning process.

4. Increasing Income: If you find it challenging to cover your expenses or make progress towards your financial goals with your current income, explore opportunities to increase your earnings. This could involve seeking a raise or promotion at your current job, acquiring new skills to enhance your employability, starting a side business or freelancing, or exploring investment opportunities. Increasing your income can provide more financial stability and flexibility.

5. Building and Protecting Credit: Your credit score plays a crucial role in your financial well-being. Establishing and maintaining good credit is important for accessing loans, favorable interest rates, and other financial opportunities. Pay your bills on time, keep your credit utilization low, and monitor your credit report regularly. If you have poor credit, take steps to improve it, such as paying off debts, disputing errors on your credit report, or seeking professional credit counseling.

6. Investing and Wealth Building: Building long-term wealth is essential for financial security and achieving your financial goals. Educate yourself about different investment options, such as stocks, bonds, real estate, or retirement accounts. Consider working with a financial advisor who can provide guidance based on your risk tolerance and financial objectives. Start investing early to benefit from compounding returns and review your investment portfolio regularly to ensure it aligns with your goals.

7. Continual Financial Education: Financial literacy is key to overcoming financial obstacles. Invest in your financial education by reading books, attending seminars or workshops, and following reputable financial resources. Stay updated on financial trends, new investment opportunities, and changes in tax laws or regulations. The more you know, the better equipped you'll be to make informed financial decisions and navigate potential challenges.

Remember, overcoming financial obstacles takes time and effort. Be patient with yourself and celebrate small victories along the way. Seek support from financial professionals, friends, or family members who can provide guidance and accountability. By taking proactive steps and maintaining a positive mindset, you can overcome financial obstacles and pave the way towards a more secure financial future.

Chapter 2

Creating a Budget

Your Path to Financial Freedom

Understanding the importance of budgeting

Budgeting is a crucial financial management tool that helps individuals, businesses, and organizations plan, track, and control their income and expenses. It involves creating a detailed plan for how money will be allocated and spent over a specific period, such as monthly, quarterly, or annually. Understanding the importance of budgeting can have numerous benefits, including:

1. Financial Discipline: Budgeting promotes discipline in managing money. It encourages individuals to prioritize their spending and make conscious decisions about how their income is allocated. By tracking expenses and sticking to a budget, people can avoid impulsive purchases, unnecessary expenses, and overspending, which can lead to financial stress and debt.

2. Goal Setting and Achievement: A budget serves as a roadmap for achieving financial goals. Whether it's saving for a down payment on a house, paying off debt, or funding a vacation, budgeting helps individuals allocate resources effectively to reach their objectives. By setting specific financial targets and monitoring progress, individuals can make informed decisions that align with their long-term aspirations.

3. Financial Awareness: Budgeting provides a clear picture of an individual's or organization's financial situation. It allows for a comprehensive overview of income sources, expenses, debts, and savings. With this knowledge, individuals can identify areas where they can cut costs, increase savings, or invest wisely. It also helps in identifying any financial leaks, such as excessive fees or unnecessary subscriptions.

4. Emergency Preparedness: Budgeting helps create an emergency fund, which is essential for handling unexpected expenses or financial setbacks. By allocating a portion of income to savings, individuals can build a cushion to handle emergencies without resorting to high-interest loans or credit card debt. Having an emergency fund provides peace of mind and financial stability during challenging times.

5. Debt Management: Budgeting plays a crucial role in managing and reducing debt. It allows individuals to allocate funds specifically for debt repayment, ensuring timely payments and avoiding late fees or penalties. By tracking debt balances and interest rates, budgeting helps prioritize high-interest debts for faster repayment, ultimately saving money on interest payments.

6. Improved Decision Making: Budgeting provides a framework for making informed financial decisions. It helps individuals evaluate the financial feasibility of major purchases or investments by considering the impact on their overall budget. By having a clear understanding of income and expenses, individuals can make well-informed choices that align with their financial priorities and long-term plans.

7. Financial Independence: Budgeting is a key tool for achieving financial independence. It empowers individuals to take control of their finances, reduce reliance on credit, and build wealth over time. By consistently following a budget and making prudent financial decisions, individuals can work towards achieving financial security and freedom.

In summary, budgeting is essential for effective financial management, enabling individuals and organizations to plan, control, and optimize their resources. It promotes financial discipline, goal achievement, awareness, emergency preparedness, debt management, improved decision making, and ultimately, financial independence.

Step-by-step guide to creating a personalized budget

Creating a personalized budget involves several steps to ensure accuracy and effectiveness. Here's a step-by-step guide to help you create your own budget:

1. Set Financial Goals: Start by determining your short-term and long-term financial goals. These could include saving for a down payment, paying off debt, creating an emergency fund, or planning for retirement. Clearly define your goals, including the amount you need and the timeline for achieving them.

2. Calculate Income: Compile all sources of income, including salary, wages, freelance work, rental income, investments, and any other sources. Determine your net income by subtracting taxes and deductions from your gross income. Use an average if your income varies from month to month.

3. Track Expenses: Track your expenses for a specific period, such as a month. Categorize your expenses into fixed expenses (e.g., rent/mortgage, utilities, insurance) and variable expenses (e.g., groceries, dining out, entertainment). Use bank statements, receipts, and expense-tracking apps to gather accurate data.

4. Analyze Current Spending: Review your expense tracking data to understand your spending patterns. Identify areas where you can potentially cut back or reduce expenses. Look for any unnecessary or discretionary expenses that can be eliminated or reduced.

5. Set Budget Categories: Create budget categories that align with your spending habits and goals. Common categories include housing, transportation, groceries, dining out, utilities, debt repayment, savings, entertainment, and personal care. Adjust the categories based on your unique needs and priorities.

6. Allocate Income: Distribute your income across the budget categories. Start with essential expenses such as housing, utilities, and debt payments. Then allocate funds to other categories based on their priority and importance. Aim to save a portion of your income for emergencies and long-term goals.

7. Be Realistic and Flexible: Ensure that your budget is realistic and achievable. Don't underestimate expenses or overestimate income. Leave room for unexpected or variable expenses. Be flexible and adjust your budget as needed to accommodate changes in income or expenses.

8. Track and Monitor: Implement a system to track and monitor your budget regularly. Use spreadsheets, budgeting apps, or online tools to record and categorize your income and expenses. Review your progress periodically to ensure you're staying on track and making adjustments as necessary.

9. Make Adjustments: As you track your budget, you may realize that certain categories need adjustments. You might find that you need to increase savings, reduce discretionary spending, or reallocate funds based on changing circumstances. Be proactive in making adjustments to ensure your budget remains effective.

10. Review and Reflect: Set aside time each month or quarter to review your budget and reflect on your financial progress. Celebrate achievements and identify areas for improvement. Use this time to reassess your goals, adjust your budget, and stay motivated to achieve financial success.

Remember, creating a personalized budget is an ongoing process. It requires discipline, regular monitoring, and adjustments as your financial situation and goals evolve. Stay committed to your budgeting efforts, and you'll gain greater control over your finances and make progress towards your financial goals.

Tips for sticking to your budget and achieving your financial goals

Sticking to a budget and achieving your financial goals can be challenging but is definitely possible with the right strategies and mindset. Here are some tips to help you stay on track and succeed:

1. Set Realistic Goals: Ensure that your financial goals are realistic and achievable within your current income and circumstances. Setting overly ambitious goals can lead to frustration and demotivation. Break larger goals into smaller milestones to track progress and celebrate achievements along the way.

2. Track Your Expenses: Continuously track and monitor your expenses to stay aware of where your money is going. Use budgeting apps, spreadsheets, or journals to record your spending. Regularly reviewing your expenses will help you identify areas where you can cut back and make adjustments to stay within your budget.

3. Prioritize Your Spending: Allocate your funds to match your priorities. Focus on essential expenses first, such as housing, utilities, and debt payments. Then allocate money towards savings, investments, and other financial goals. Be mindful of discretionary expenses and consider whether they align with your priorities or if they can be reduced.

4. Use Cash Envelopes or Digital Budgeting Tools: Consider using the cash envelope system, where you allocate a specific amount of cash for each spending category. This physical separation can help you visualize and control your spending. Alternatively, utilize digital budgeting tools and apps that automate tracking, categorization, and provide spending alerts.

5. Avoid Impulse Buying: Practice self-discipline and avoid impulsive purchases. Before making a purchase, ask yourself if it aligns with your budget and financial goals. Consider implementing a waiting period, such as 24 hours, before making non-essential purchases. This gives you time to evaluate whether it's a necessary expense or a fleeting desire.

6. Find Frugal Alternatives: Look for cost-effective alternatives and frugal habits that can help you save money. For example, meal planning and cooking at home instead of dining out, using public transportation or carpooling instead of driving alone, or shopping for discounts and using coupons. Small changes can add up over time and have a significant impact on your budget.

7. Stay Motivated: Remind yourself of the financial goals you are working towards and the benefits of sticking to your budget. Create visual reminders or vision boards that represent your goals. Surround yourself with supportive individuals who understand and encourage your financial journey. Celebrate milestones and achievements along the way to stay motivated.

8. Prepare for Unexpected Expenses: Set aside funds for emergencies and unexpected expenses in your budget. Having an emergency fund ensures you don't have to rely on credit cards or loans when faced with unexpected financial challenges. It provides a safety net and peace of mind, allowing you to stay on track with your budget.

9. Review and Adjust Regularly: Review your budget regularly to assess your progress and make necessary adjustments. Life circumstances change, and your budget should adapt accordingly. If you encounter challenges or unexpected changes, be flexible and adjust your budget as needed while keeping your long-term goals in mind.

10. Seek Support and Education: Take advantage of financial resources and educational materials available to you. Attend workshops or webinars on personal finance, read books or articles, or consult with financial advisors. The more knowledge and support you have, the better equipped you'll be to stick to your budget and achieve your financial goals.

Remember that sticking to a budget is a continuous process that requires discipline and commitment. Stay focused, be patient with yourself, and celebrate each step forward. With perseverance and dedication, you can achieve financial stability and reach your financial goals.

Chapter 3

Mastering Debt

Strategies to Conquer and Thrive

Differentiating between good and bad debt

Differentiating between good debt and bad debt is important in making informed financial decisions. While debt is generally associated with negative connotations, not all debt is inherently bad. Here's how you can distinguish between the two:

Good Debt:
1. Investment in Assets: Good debt is incurred when the borrowed funds are used to acquire assets that have the potential to appreciate in value or generate income over time. For example, taking a mortgage to purchase a home or obtaining a loan to start a business.

2. Low Interest Rates: Good debt typically comes with lower interest rates compared to bad debt. This allows borrowers to pay off the debt more easily and can be leveraged to create wealth or improve financial stability.

3. Potential Tax Benefits: Some types of debt, such as mortgage interest or student loan interest, may offer tax deductions or credits, reducing the overall cost of borrowing. These tax benefits can make the debt more manageable and financially advantageous.

4. Positive Impact on Credit Score: Good debt, when managed responsibly, can positively impact your credit score. Consistently making payments on time and as agreed demonstrates your ability to handle credit responsibly, leading to better borrowing opportunities and favorable interest rates in the future.

5. Long-Term Value: Good debt is often associated with investments that have long-term value and can contribute to your financial well-being. Examples include education, real estate, or business ventures that have the potential to generate income or appreciation over time.

Bad Debt:

1. High-Interest Rates: Bad debt typically carries high interest rates, making it more costly to repay over time. This includes credit card debt, payday loans, or high-interest personal loans. The high interest charges can lead to a cycle of debt that is difficult to break.

2. Consumer Spending: Bad debt is often accumulated through discretionary spending on non-essential items or services that do not retain or appreciate in value. This includes luxury items, vacations, dining out excessively, or impulse purchases that are financed through credit.

3. No Potential for Return on Investment: Unlike good debt, bad debt does not provide any potential for return on investment. It represents borrowing for items or experiences that do not contribute to your long-term financial stability or wealth creation.

4. Negative Impact on Credit Score: Failure to manage bad debt responsibly can have a detrimental impact on your credit score. Late payments, defaults, or high credit utilization can lower your credit score, making it harder to obtain favorable terms on future loans or credit.

5. Financial Stress: Accumulating excessive bad debt can lead to financial stress and limited financial freedom. High debt burdens can restrict your ability to save, invest, or achieve other financial goals, ultimately hindering your financial well-being.

It's essential to assess your financial situation, evaluate the purpose of the debt, and consider the potential benefits and risks before taking on any debt. While good debt can be used strategically to build wealth and improve your financial position, it's important to minimize or avoid bad debt that can hinder your financial progress.

Effective methods for debt management and reduction

Debt management and reduction require discipline, strategic planning, and consistent effort. Here are some effective methods to help you manage and reduce your debt:

1. Create a Debt Repayment Plan: Start by organizing your debts, listing them by interest rate, outstanding balance, and minimum monthly payment. Prioritize high-interest debts, as they cost you the most in interest over time. Consider using the debt snowball or debt avalanche method to determine the order in which you'll tackle your debts.

2. Budgeting and Expense Tracking: Create a realistic budget that allows you to allocate a portion of your income towards debt repayment. Track your expenses diligently to identify areas where you can cut back and allocate more funds towards debt repayment. By optimizing your spending habits, you can free up more money to put towards paying off your debts.

3. Make Extra Payments: Whenever possible, make extra payments towards your debts. Even small additional payments can make a significant impact over time. Consider using windfalls like tax refunds, bonuses, or cash gifts to make lump sum payments towards your debts. Be sure to communicate with your lenders to ensure the extra payments are applied correctly towards the principal balance.

4. Debt Consolidation: If you have multiple high-interest debts, consider consolidating them into a single loan with a lower interest rate. This can simplify your debt management by combining your debts into one payment. It may also lower your overall interest expenses, making it easier to pay off your debts faster.

5. Negotiate with Creditors: If you're struggling to meet your debt obligations, contact your creditors to discuss possible options. They may be willing to negotiate a lower interest rate, modify your repayment terms, or offer a hardship program. Exploring these options can provide temporary relief or better terms for debt repayment.

6. Increase Income: Look for ways to increase your income to accelerate your debt repayment efforts. This can include taking on a part-time job, freelancing, selling unused items, or exploring side hustles. The extra income can be directly applied towards paying off your debts, allowing you to make more substantial progress.

7. Seek Professional Help: If you're overwhelmed with debt or struggling to manage your payments, consider seeking assistance from a reputable credit counseling agency or financial advisor. They can provide personalized guidance, help negotiate with creditors, and develop a debt management plan tailored to your specific situation.

8. Avoid Taking on New Debt: While working towards debt reduction, it's important to avoid accumulating new debt. Minimize or eliminate the use of credit cards and focus on living within your means. This will prevent further debt accumulation and allow you to direct more resources towards paying off existing debts.

9. Stay Motivated and Celebrate Milestones: Debt reduction is a journey that requires persistence and motivation. Set realistic milestones and celebrate your achievements along the way. Rewarding yourself periodically for reaching milestones can help maintain your focus and commitment to debt repayment.

10. Educate Yourself on Personal Finance: Invest time in learning about personal finance, debt management strategies, and financial literacy. Understanding the principles of money management will empower you to make informed decisions and develop healthy financial habits for the long term.

Remember, managing and reducing debt takes time and effort. Stay committed to your debt repayment plan, be patient with the process, and celebrate each milestone you achieve. Over time, diligent debt management will lead to improved financial well-being and ultimately, debt freedom.

Developing a plan to eliminate debt and build a debt-free future

Developing a plan to eliminate debt and build a debt-free future requires careful planning, discipline, and perseverance. Here are the steps to help you create a comprehensive debt elimination plan:

1. Assess Your Current Debt Situation: Start by gathering all the necessary information about your debts, including outstanding balances, interest rates, minimum monthly payments, and any other relevant details. List your debts in order, starting from the highest interest rate to the lowest.

2. Set Clear Debt Elimination Goals: Define your debt elimination goals, including the total amount of debt you want to eliminate and a target timeline. Make sure your goals are realistic and achievable based on your financial situation.

3. Review Your Budget: Evaluate your current income, expenses, and spending habits. Create a detailed budget that prioritizes debt repayment. Identify areas where you can cut back or reduce expenses to allocate more funds toward debt repayment.

4. Choose a Debt Repayment Strategy: There are two common strategies to consider: the Debt Snowball Method and the Debt Avalanche Method.

- Debt Snowball Method: Start by paying off the debt with the lowest balance while making minimum payments on all other debts. Once the first debt is paid off, move on to the next lowest balance, and so on. This method provides psychological motivation as you see debts being eliminated.

- Debt Avalanche Method: Focus on paying off debts with the highest interest rates first while making minimum payments on other debts. Once the highest interest debt is paid off, move

on to the next highest interest debt. This method saves more money on interest payments over time.

Choose the strategy that aligns best with your financial goals and motivates you to stay committed.

5. Negotiate with Creditors: Reach out to your creditors to explore possible options for lower interest rates, payment plans, or debt settlement agreements. Negotiating with creditors can help ease your financial burden and make it more manageable to pay off your debts.

6. Increase Income and Reduce Expenses: Consider ways to increase your income to accelerate your debt repayment efforts. This can include taking on a side job, freelancing, or selling unused items. Additionally, continue to find ways to reduce expenses by cutting back on discretionary spending and identifying areas where you can save.

7. Implement the Debt Repayment Plan: Put your debt repayment plan into action. Make minimum payments on all debts while allocating extra funds toward the debt with the highest priority (based on your chosen repayment strategy). As each debt is paid off, roll the payments into the next debt until all debts are cleared.

8. Stay Motivated and Track Progress: Debt elimination requires time and dedication. Stay motivated by regularly tracking your progress and celebrating milestones along the way. Consider using debt repayment tracking tools or apps to visualize your progress and keep you motivated.

9. Avoid Taking on New Debt: As you work toward becoming debt-free, avoid taking on new debt. Minimize or eliminate the use of credit cards and focus on living within your means. This will prevent you from falling back into a cycle of debt.

10. Build an Emergency Fund and Save for the Future: Once your debts are paid off, allocate the funds previously used for debt repayment to build an emergency fund. Aim for 3-6 months' worth of living expenses to cover unexpected financial emergencies. Additionally, start saving for future goals such as retirement, education, or homeownership.

Remember, eliminating debt and building a debt-free future requires persistence and consistency. Be patient with the process, stay committed to your plan, and celebrate each step forward. With determination, discipline, and a well-executed debt elimination plan, you can achieve a debt-free future and regain control of your financial well-being.

Part 2
Growing Wealth in the Digital Era

Chapter 4

Investment Essentials

A Comprehensive Guide for Beginners

Understanding investment vehicles and options

Investment vehicles and options refer to the various instruments and methods available to individuals for investing their money with the goal of generating returns and growing their wealth. Here are some common investment vehicles and options:

1. Stocks: Stocks represent ownership shares in a company. Investing in stocks allows individuals to participate in the company's growth and share in its profits through capital appreciation and dividends. Stocks can be purchased through individual company shares or exchange-traded funds (ETFs).

2. Bonds: Bonds are debt securities issued by governments, municipalities, or corporations to raise capital. When you invest in bonds, you are essentially lending money to the issuer in exchange for regular interest payments and the return of the principal amount at maturity. Bonds are considered relatively lower-risk investments compared to stocks.

3. Mutual Funds: Mutual funds pool money from multiple investors to invest in a diversified portfolio of stocks, bonds, or other assets. They are managed by professional fund managers who make investment decisions on behalf of the investors. Mutual funds offer diversification and are suitable for individuals seeking professional management and broader market exposure.

4. Exchange-Traded Funds (ETFs): ETFs are similar to mutual funds but trade on stock exchanges like individual stocks. ETFs can track various indices, sectors, commodities, or asset classes. They offer diversification, flexibility, and intra-day trading. ETFs are also known for their relatively lower expense ratios compared to mutual funds.

5. Real Estate Investment Trusts (REITs): REITs are investment vehicles that own and operate income-generating real estate properties. By investing in REITs, individuals can gain exposure to the real estate market without directly owning physical properties. REITs distribute a significant portion of their earnings as dividends to investors.

6. Commodities: Commodities include physical goods like gold, silver, oil, natural gas, agricultural products, etc. Investing in commodities can be done through futures contracts, commodity-specific funds, or exchange-traded products (ETPs). Commodities can serve as a hedge against inflation or provide diversification in an investment portfolio.

7. Index Funds: Index funds are a type of mutual fund or ETF that aims to replicate the performance of a specific market index, such as the S&P 500. They offer broad market exposure and are often passively managed, meaning they seek to track the index rather than actively selecting individual securities.

8. Options and Futures: Options and futures are derivative contracts that provide individuals with the right or obligation to buy or sell an underlying asset at a predetermined price and date. These instruments are often used for hedging, speculation, or managing risk in investment portfolios. However, they can be complex and require a good understanding of the market.

9. Certificates of Deposit (CDs): CDs are time deposits offered by banks and financial institutions. They offer a fixed interest rate and maturity date. Investing in CDs provides a relatively safe and predictable return, making them suitable for individuals seeking capital preservation and a fixed income stream.

10. Peer-to-Peer Lending (P2P): P2P lending platforms connect borrowers with lenders, bypassing traditional financial institutions. As an investor, you can lend money to individuals or small businesses and earn interest on your investment. P2P lending offers potentially higher returns but comes with higher risk compared to traditional fixed-income investments.

It's important to note that each investment vehicle comes with its own risks, rewards, and suitability based on individual goals, risk tolerance, and time horizon. Before investing, it is advisable to conduct thorough research, consider diversification, and, if needed, consult with a financial advisor to make informed investment decisions.

Risk management and diversification strategies

Risk management and diversification are crucial strategies for managing investment portfolios effectively. Here are some key principles and strategies to consider:

1. Diversification: Diversification involves spreading your investments across different asset classes, sectors, regions, and investment vehicles. By diversifying, you aim to reduce the impact of any single investment's performance on your overall portfolio. Diversification can be achieved through a combination of the following:

- *Asset Allocation:* Allocate your investments across different asset classes, such as stocks, bonds, real estate, and commodities, based on your risk tolerance, investment goals, and time horizon. This helps to balance risk and potential returns.

- *Sector Allocation:* Invest in various sectors, such as technology, healthcare, financial services, consumer goods, etc., to reduce exposure to any single industry's specific risks.

- *Geographic Allocation:* Consider investing in companies or assets across different countries and regions to mitigate the impact of local economic or political factors.

- *Investment Vehicles:* Spread your investments across different types of investment vehicles, such as mutual funds, ETFs, individual stocks, bonds, and alternative investments.

2. Risk Assessment and Tolerance: Assess your risk tolerance by understanding your financial goals, time horizon, and ability to withstand fluctuations in investment values. This assessment helps determine the appropriate level of risk you can comfortably tolerate. Consider factors such as age, financial obligations, income stability, and long-term goals.

3. Asset Allocation: Determine an appropriate asset allocation that aligns with your risk tolerance and investment objectives. The right asset allocation takes into account your risk appetite, time horizon, and expected returns. Typically, a more aggressive portfolio may have a higher allocation to stocks, while a conservative portfolio may have a higher allocation to bonds or cash.

4. Regular Portfolio Review: Regularly review and rebalance your portfolio to maintain your desired asset allocation. Over time, the performance of different assets can deviate from the original allocation, leading to an imbalance. Rebalancing involves selling overperforming assets and buying underperforming assets to bring the portfolio back to its target allocation.

5. Risk Mitigation Strategies: Consider using risk mitigation strategies to protect your portfolio from potential downside risks. These strategies include:

- ***Stop-Loss Orders:*** Set predetermined price points at which you would sell an investment if it reaches a certain level, limiting potential losses.

- ***Hedging:*** Use financial instruments like options, futures, or short selling to offset potential losses in specific investments or sectors.

- ***Dollar-Cost Averaging:*** Invest a fixed amount of money regularly, regardless of market conditions. This strategy helps smooth out the impact of market volatility by buying more shares when prices are low and fewer shares when prices are high.

- Asset-Class Diversification: Diversify within each asset class. For example, in stocks, diversify across different sectors, company sizes, and geographies.

6. Risk and Market Research: Stay informed about market trends, economic indicators, and the performance of individual investments. Conduct thorough research and analysis before making investment decisions. Stay up to date with news, financial statements, industry reports, and expert opinions to make informed choices.

7. Professional Advice: If needed, seek guidance from a financial advisor or investment professional who can help you assess your risk profile, develop an appropriate investment strategy, and provide ongoing portfolio management.

Remember, while diversification and risk management can help mitigate investment risks, they do not guarantee profits or protect against all losses. It's important to continuously monitor and assess your investments and adjust your strategies as needed based on changing market conditions, personal circumstances, and financial goals.

Tips for selecting the right investments for your financial goals

Selecting the right investments for your financial goals requires careful consideration and alignment with your objectives, risk tolerance, and time horizon. Here are some tips to help you make informed investment decisions:

1. Define Your Financial Goals: Clearly identify your financial goals, whether it's saving for retirement, buying a home, funding education, or achieving long-term wealth accumulation. Determine the timeframe for each goal, as it will influence your investment strategy.

2. Assess Your Risk Tolerance: Evaluate your risk tolerance by considering factors such as your age, financial obligations, income stability, and comfort level with market fluctuations. Understand how much risk you are willing and able to take to achieve your goals.

3. Consider Time Horizon: Differentiate between short-term and long-term goals. Short-term goals typically have a horizon of fewer than five years, while long-term goals span over five years or more. Longer time horizons generally allow for a higher allocation to growth-oriented investments like stocks.

4. Diversify Your Portfolio: Embrace diversification by spreading your investments across various asset classes, sectors, and regions. Diversification helps reduce risk by not relying heavily on any single investment. It can be achieved through asset allocation, sector allocation, geographic allocation, and the use of different investment vehicles.

5. Conduct Research: Perform thorough research on potential investments. Analyze factors such as historical performance, financial health of the company or issuer, industry trends, competitive positioning, and management track record. Evaluate risks, growth prospects, and any regulatory or macroeconomic factors that may impact the investment.

6. Understand Investment Vehicles: Gain a comprehensive understanding of the investment vehicles available to you, such as stocks, bonds, mutual funds, ETFs, real estate, or commodities. Know their characteristics, risk-reward profiles, fees, and tax implications. Choose investments that align with your goals and risk tolerance.

7. Seek Professional Advice: If you lack the necessary expertise or time to research and manage investments, consider seeking guidance from a financial advisor or investment professional. They can provide personalized advice based on your financial situation, goals, and risk tolerance.

8. Monitor and Review: Regularly monitor your investments and review their performance relative to your goals. Assess whether they are on track or require adjustments. Stay informed about market trends, economic indicators, and any changes that may impact your investments.

9. Consider Cost and Fees: Pay attention to the costs associated with investments, including management fees, commissions, expense ratios, and transaction costs. High costs can eat into your returns over time, so choose investments with reasonable fees or explore lower-cost options like index funds or ETFs.

10. Stay Disciplined: Stick to your investment plan and avoid making emotional or impulsive decisions based on short-term market fluctuations. Maintain a long-term perspective and focus on the fundamentals of your investments and their alignment with your financial goals.

Remember, investing involves risks, and there is no guaranteed outcome. Make informed decisions based on your unique circumstances, goals, and risk tolerance. Regularly review and adjust your investments as needed to stay on track towards achieving your financial objectives.

Chapter 5

Digital Investment Platforms

Maximizing Returns with Technology

Exploring the advantages of digital investment platforms

Digital investment platforms, also known as online investment platforms or robo-advisors, offer several advantages for investors. Here are some of the key advantages of using digital investment platforms:

1. Accessibility and Convenience: Digital investment platforms provide easy access to investment opportunities anytime, anywhere. You can manage your investments through user-friendly web or mobile interfaces, allowing you to monitor and make changes to your portfolio at your convenience.

2. Lower Costs: Digital investment platforms often have lower fees compared to traditional investment services. By utilizing technology and automation, they can provide cost-effective investment solutions. This is particularly beneficial for smaller investors who may not have access to expensive investment products or services.

3. Diversification and Risk Management: Many digital investment platforms offer diversified portfolios that are designed to manage risk based on your risk profile and investment goals. Through automated algorithms, these platforms allocate your investments across various asset classes, sectors, and regions to achieve diversification and help reduce risk.

4. Personalized Investment Advice: Digital investment platforms typically offer personalized investment advice based on your risk tolerance, financial goals, and time horizon. They use sophisticated algorithms and questionnaires to assess your risk profile and recommend suitable investment portfolios.

5. Transparency and Control: Digital investment platforms provide transparency in terms of investment holdings, performance, and fees. You can easily track your investments and understand the underlying assets in your portfolio. This transparency gives you a clear view of how your investments are performing and allows you to make informed decisions.

6. Automation and Rebalancing: Digital investment platforms automate investment processes such as portfolio rebalancing. They regularly monitor your portfolio and adjust the allocation to maintain the desired asset allocation. This automation helps ensure that your portfolio remains aligned with your risk profile and investment objectives without requiring constant manual intervention.

7. Educational Resources: Many digital investment platforms offer educational resources, such as articles, webinars, or tools, to help investors learn about investing and make informed decisions. These resources can be particularly valuable for individuals who are new to investing or want to enhance their knowledge.

8. Scalability: Digital investment platforms can cater to a wide range of investors, from beginners to experienced individuals. They offer scalable solutions that can accommodate different investment amounts and goals. As your investment portfolio grows, these platforms can adjust the investment strategy accordingly.

9. Customer Support: Digital investment platforms typically provide customer support through various channels, including email, chat, or phone. Although the support may be digital rather than in-person, it can still be responsive and helpful in addressing any questions or concerns you may have.

10. Integration with Financial Tools: Many digital investment platforms integrate with other financial tools or apps, allowing you to have a comprehensive view of your financial situation. They can sync with budgeting tools, financial planning software, or personal finance apps, providing a holistic view of your financial health.

While digital investment platforms offer numerous advantages, it's essential to consider your specific needs, investment goals, and comfort level with technology. Evaluate different platforms based on their features, fees, investment options, and customer reviews to choose one that aligns with your preferences and investment objectives.

Step-by-step guide to getting started with online investing

Getting started with online investing can seem overwhelming, but with the right approach, it can be a straightforward process. Here's a step-by-step guide to help you get started with online investing:

1. Define Your Investment Goals: Clearly define your investment goals, whether it's saving for retirement, a down payment on a house, or building long-term wealth. Determine your time horizon for each goal, as it will influence your investment strategy.

2. Assess Your Risk Tolerance: Evaluate your risk tolerance by considering factors such as your age, financial obligations, income stability, and comfort level with market fluctuations. Understand how much risk you are willing and able to take to achieve your goals.

3. Research Online Investment Platforms: Explore different online investment platforms, also known as robo-advisors, and compare their features, fees, investment options, and customer reviews. Consider factors such as account minimums, fee structures, investment strategies, and available support.

4. Choose the Right Platform: Select an online investment platform that aligns with your investment goals, risk tolerance, and preferences. Consider factors such as diversification, cost-effectiveness, transparency, ease of use, and the level of customer support provided.

5. Open an Account: Once you've chosen an online investment platform, visit their website and open an account. You'll typically need to provide personal information, such as your name, address, social security number, and employment details. The platform may also ask you to complete a questionnaire to assess your risk profile.

6. Determine Your Investment Strategy: Based on your investment goals, risk tolerance, and the information provided in the risk assessment questionnaire, the online investment platform will recommend an investment strategy for you. This may involve a recommended asset allocation and portfolio composition.

7. Fund Your Account: To start investing, fund your online investment account. Most platforms offer various funding options, such as bank transfers, wire transfers, or linking your existing bank accounts. Follow the platform's instructions for depositing funds into your investment account.

8. Select and Customize Your Portfolio: Once your account is funded, you'll typically have the option to choose a pre-set portfolio based on your recommended investment strategy or customize your own portfolio. Select the investment approach that aligns with your preferences and review the underlying investments in your portfolio.

9. Review and Confirm: Before finalizing your investment, carefully review the details of your selected portfolio, including the asset allocation, investment holdings, fees, and any additional investment features. Ensure everything is accurate and meets your expectations.

10. Monitor and Adjust: After your investments are made, regularly monitor your portfolio's performance and review your investment strategy periodically. Stay informed about market trends, economic indicators, and any changes that may impact your investments. Consider rebalancing your portfolio if necessary to maintain your desired asset allocation.

Remember, investing involves risks, and there are no guarantees of returns. Stay focused on your long-term goals, avoid making impulsive decisions based on short-term market fluctuations, and seek professional advice if needed. As you gain more experience and confidence, you can continue to educate yourself and refine your investment strategy.

Analyzing investment trends and leveraging technology for informed decisions

Analyzing investment trends and leveraging technology for informed decisions is an effective approach to enhancing investment strategies. By staying abreast of market trends and utilizing technology-driven tools, investors can make more informed decisions that may lead to better returns. Here are some key steps and considerations to follow:

1. Stay updated on investment trends: Regularly monitor and analyze market trends to identify potential investment opportunities. Utilize financial news outlets, industry publications, and online resources to gather information about emerging sectors, innovative technologies, and global economic developments.

2. Leverage data analytics: Utilize data analytics tools and platforms to process and interpret vast amounts of financial data. By analyzing historical data, market patterns, and key performance indicators, investors can identify potential trends, correlations, and investment opportunities.

3. Implement AI and machine learning: Explore the benefits of artificial intelligence (AI) and machine learning algorithms in investment analysis. These technologies can help identify patterns, predict market movements, and automate investment strategies. AI-powered platforms can also provide real-time insights, risk assessments, and portfolio optimization suggestions.

4. Use robo-advisors: Robo-advisory services leverage technology to offer automated investment advice. These platforms use algorithms and client-specific inputs to create diversified portfolios, manage risk, and optimize asset allocation. Robo-advisors provide low-cost and user-friendly investment solutions, particularly for individuals with limited investment experience.

5. Explore alternative data sources: In addition to traditional financial data, consider incorporating alternative data sources into investment analysis. Alternative data refers to non-traditional information such as social media sentiment, web scraping data, satellite imagery, and supply chain analytics. Analyzing alternative data can provide unique insights and potentially uncover hidden investment opportunities.

6. Risk management tools: Utilize risk management tools to assess and mitigate investment risks. These tools help evaluate portfolio volatility, stress testing, and scenario analysis. By understanding potential risks, investors can make informed decisions and develop strategies to protect their investments.

7. Embrace blockchain and cryptocurrencies: Stay informed about developments in blockchain technology and cryptocurrencies. Blockchain offers enhanced security, transparency, and efficiency in financial transactions. Cryptocurrencies can provide investment diversification opportunities, but thorough research and risk management are crucial due to their volatility and regulatory uncertainties.

8. Continuous learning and adaptability: Investment trends and technology are constantly evolving, so it's essential to stay curious and continuously update your knowledge. Participate in industry events, attend webinars, join investment forums, and engage with like-minded professionals to share insights and ideas.

Remember that while technology and data-driven analysis can be valuable tools, they should be used in conjunction with a well-rounded investment strategy. Factors such as fundamental analysis, risk tolerance, diversification, and long-term goals should also be considered when making investment decisions.

Chapter 6

Building Retirement Security

Planning for the Future You Desire

Navigating retirement savings options (401(k), IRA, etc.)

Navigating retirement savings options can be overwhelming, but understanding the basics of popular retirement accounts like 401(k) and IRA can help you make informed decisions. Here's an overview of these options:

1. 401(k) plans:

  - Offered by employers to their employees.

  - Contributions are deducted from your salary before taxes, reducing your taxable income.

  - Employers may offer a matching contribution up to a certain percentage of your salary.

  - Contributions and investment earnings grow tax-deferred until withdrawal.

- Withdrawals are generally subject to income tax and penalties if taken before age 59 ½, except for specific circumstances like hardship withdrawals.

- Contribution limits are set annually by the IRS.

2. Traditional IRAs (Individual Retirement Accounts):

- Available to anyone with earned income.

- Contributions are typically tax-deductible, reducing your taxable income.

- Investments in the IRA grow tax-deferred until withdrawal.

- Withdrawals are generally subject to income tax and penalties if taken before age 59 ½, except for specific circumstances like first-time homebuyer expenses or qualified education expenses.

- Contribution limits are set annually by the IRS.

3. Roth IRAs:

- Available to individuals meeting income eligibility requirements.

- Contributions are made with after-tax dollars, so they are not tax-deductible.

- Investments in the Roth IRA grow tax-free.

- Qualified withdrawals, including both contributions and earnings, are tax-free.

- Contributions can be withdrawn penalty-free at any time, while earnings may be subject to penalties if withdrawn before age 59 ½, except for specific circumstances like qualified first-time homebuyer expenses or qualified education expenses.

- Contribution limits are set annually by the IRS.

4. Simplified Employee Pension (SEP) IRAs:

- Designed for self-employed individuals and small business owners.

- Contributions are made by the employer, and the maximum contribution is a percentage of the employee's compensation or a fixed dollar amount, whichever is less.

- Employer contributions are tax-deductible.

- Withdrawals are generally subject to income tax and penalties if taken before age 59 ½, except for specific circumstances.

- Contribution limits are higher compared to Traditional and Roth IRAs.

5. Solo 401(k) or Individual 401(k):

- Designed for self-employed individuals with no employees, or for those with a spouse who is also involved in the business.

- Allows for both employer and employee contributions, providing higher contribution limits compared to SEP IRAs.

- Contributions are tax-deductible for the employer, and employee contributions can be made on a pre-tax or Roth basis.

- Withdrawals are subject to income tax and penalties if taken before age 59 ½, except for specific circumstances.

- Contribution limits are set annually by the IRS.

When deciding which retirement savings options to utilize, consider factors such as eligibility, contribution limits, tax advantages, employer matches (for 401(k)), investment options, and withdrawal rules. It's also a good idea to consult with a financial advisor or tax professional who can provide personalized guidance based on your specific circumstances and retirement goals.

Strategies to accelerate retirement savings

Accelerating retirement savings requires a proactive approach and disciplined saving habits. Here are some strategies to help you boost your retirement savings:

1. Start early: The power of compounding works best over a long time horizon. The earlier you start saving for retirement, the more time your investments have to grow. Even small contributions made consistently over many years can make a significant difference.

2. Maximize employer contributions: If your employer offers a 401(k) or similar retirement plan with a matching contribution, take full advantage of it. Contribute at least enough to receive the maximum matching amount, as it's essentially free money that can significantly enhance your retirement savings.

3. Increase your savings rate: Aim to save a higher percentage of your income each year. If possible, gradually increase your contribution rate to your retirement accounts. Even a small increase can have a significant impact over time.

4. Take advantage of catch-up contributions: If you're 50 years old or older, you can make additional catch-up contributions to certain retirement accounts. For example, in 2023, individuals aged 50 or older can make catch-up contributions of up to $6,500 to their 401(k) plans and up to $1,000 to IRAs.

5. Prioritize tax-advantaged accounts: Maximize contributions to tax-advantaged retirement accounts like 401(k)s and IRAs. These accounts offer tax advantages such as tax-deferred growth or tax-free withdrawals (in the case of Roth accounts), allowing your savings to compound more efficiently.

6. Automate your savings: Set up automatic contributions to your retirement accounts directly from your paycheck or bank account. This ensures consistent savings and removes the temptation to spend the money elsewhere.

7. Cut expenses and increase savings: Review your budget and identify areas where you can reduce expenses. This could involve cutting unnecessary costs, renegotiating bills, or finding ways to save on everyday expenses. Allocate the savings to your retirement accounts.

8. Diversify your investments: Build a diversified investment portfolio tailored to your risk tolerance and long-term goals. Diversification helps spread risk and potentially enhance returns. Consider a mix of stocks, bonds, and other assets based on your investment horizon and risk tolerance.

9. Minimize investment fees: High fees can eat into your returns over time. Review the expense ratios and management fees of your investment funds and consider low-cost index funds or exchange-traded funds (ETFs) as they tend to have lower fees compared to actively managed funds.

10. Continuously monitor and adjust your strategy: Regularly review your retirement savings plan and make adjustments as needed. Monitor your investment performance, rebalance your portfolio periodically, and stay informed about changes in tax laws and retirement account rules that may affect your savings strategy.

Remember, everyone's financial situation is unique, so it's important to personalize these strategies based on your goals, risk tolerance, and individual circumstances. Consulting with a financial advisor can provide additional guidance tailored to your specific needs.

Planning for retirement lifestyle and longevity

Planning for retirement lifestyle and longevity involves considering factors such as your desired lifestyle, healthcare costs, and the potential length of your retirement. Here are some key considerations:

1. Determine your retirement goals: Start by envisioning the lifestyle you want to have in retirement. Consider factors such as where you want to live, travel plans, hobbies, and any other activities you wish to pursue. Having a clear vision of your retirement goals will help you estimate the funds needed to support that lifestyle.

2. Estimate your retirement expenses: Create a detailed budget that outlines your expected expenses in retirement. Include essentials like housing, healthcare, food, and utilities, as well as discretionary expenses like travel, entertainment, and hobbies. Consider inflation when projecting future expenses. This estimation will give you an idea of the income you'll need during retirement.

3. Assess healthcare costs: Healthcare expenses tend to increase as you age. Research the cost of health insurance, long-term care insurance, and potential out-of-pocket expenses such as prescription medications, doctor visits, and medical procedures. Consider how these costs may impact your retirement savings and explore options for mitigating healthcare expenses.

4. Understand retirement income sources: Identify and understand your potential sources of retirement income. These may include Social Security benefits, pension plans (if applicable), and investment income from retirement accounts. Calculate the estimated income you'll receive from these sources and assess if it's sufficient to cover your projected expenses.

5. Save and invest strategically: Maximize your savings during your working years. Contribute regularly to retirement accounts like 401(k)s and IRAs and take advantage of any employer matching programs. Consider a diversified investment strategy that aligns with your risk tolerance and retirement timeline. Revisit and adjust your investment portfolio periodically to ensure it remains aligned with your goals.

6. Plan for longevity: With advancements in healthcare and increased life expectancy, it's crucial to plan for a potentially longer retirement period. Consider the average life expectancy, your family's health history, and your lifestyle choices. Saving and investing with the expectation of a longer retirement can help ensure you have sufficient funds to sustain your desired lifestyle.

7. Consider working part-time: If you're comfortable and able to do so, consider working part-time during retirement. This can help supplement your retirement income, provide social engagement, and potentially delay drawing from your retirement savings, allowing them to grow further.

8. Review and adjust your plan: Regularly review and update your retirement plan as circumstances change. Revisit your goals, adjust your budget, and assess the progress of your retirement savings. Seek professional advice from financial planners or advisors who can provide guidance and help you make informed decisions.

Remember, retirement planning is a dynamic process, and it's important to regularly reassess your goals, finances, and assumptions. By taking a proactive approach and regularly reviewing your plan, you can better align your retirement savings with your desired lifestyle and potential longevity.

Part 3
Thriving in the Digital Economy

Chapter 7

Side Hustles and Freelancing

Unlocking Additional Streams of Income

Exploring the gig economy and freelance opportunities

Exploring the gig economy and freelance opportunities can provide flexibility, independence, and the potential to earn income on your own terms. Here are some key points to consider when venturing into the gig economy:

1. Identify your skills and interests: Assess your strengths, expertise, and interests to identify the types of freelance work or gig opportunities that align with your capabilities. This could include areas such as writing, graphic design, web development, consulting, tutoring, or driving, among many others.

2. Research platforms and marketplaces: Explore various online platforms and marketplaces that connect freelancers with clients or offer gig opportunities. Examples include Upwork, Fiverr, Freelancer, TaskRabbit, Uber, Lyft, and Airbnb. Research the platforms to understand their fees, client base, competition, and overall reputation.

3. Build a portfolio or online presence: Depending on the type of freelance work you're pursuing, consider building a portfolio or creating an online presence to showcase your skills and previous work. This could include a personal website, social media profiles, or a portfolio platform specific to your industry.

4. Network and leverage connections: Utilize your professional network and connections to find potential freelance opportunities. Reach out to colleagues, former employers, and industry contacts who may be aware of freelance work or can refer you to potential clients.

5. Set competitive pricing: Research the prevailing rates for your type of freelance work to ensure your pricing is competitive. Consider factors such as your experience, skill level, and the value you provide to clients. As you gain more experience and positive reviews, you can gradually increase your rates.

6. Maintain a professional approach: Treat freelancing as a business and maintain a professional approach. Clearly communicate with clients, establish expectations, meet deadlines, and provide high-quality work. Building a positive reputation and delivering exceptional service can lead to repeat business and positive referrals.

7. Manage finances and taxes: As a freelancer or gig worker, you'll be responsible for managing your finances and tracking your income and expenses. Set up a separate bank account for your business, keep detailed records of your earnings and expenses, and consult with a tax professional to understand your tax obligations and potential deductions.

8. Continuously develop your skills: Invest in your professional development by staying updated on industry trends, learning new skills, and expanding your knowledge base. This will enhance your expertise and increase your marketability in the gig economy.

9. Plan for income variability: Freelance income can vary from month to month, so it's important to plan for fluctuations in your earnings. Create a budget that accounts for both high and low-income periods, and establish an emergency fund to provide a financial safety net.

10. Balance work-life integration: While the gig economy offers flexibility, it's essential to establish boundaries and maintain a healthy work-life balance. Set clear working hours, prioritize self-care, and avoid overcommitting yourself to ensure sustainable productivity and well-being.

Remember that the gig economy may require some time and effort to establish yourself and build a client base. Persistence, professionalism, and a continuous focus on improving your skills and services can lead to long-term success in the freelance world.

Turning hobbies and passions into profitable side ventures

Turning hobbies and passions into profitable side ventures can be an exciting and fulfilling way to earn income. Here are some steps to consider when transforming your hobbies into successful side businesses:

1. Identify your passion and market demand: Assess your hobbies and interests to identify areas where you have both a passion and market demand. Look for niches or gaps in the market that align with your skills and expertise.

2. Research the market and competition: Conduct thorough market research to understand the demand, competition, and potential customers for your product or service. Identify your target audience, study competitors' offerings, and assess pricing, marketing strategies, and customer preferences.

3. Determine your unique value proposition: Define what makes your hobby-based venture stand out from competitors. Identify your unique selling points, whether it's personalized service, exceptional quality, unique designs, or specialized knowledge. Differentiating yourself will help attract customers and build a loyal following.

4. Develop a business plan: Create a business plan outlining your goals, target market, marketing strategies, pricing, financial projections, and growth plans. A well-thought-out plan will guide your decision-making and provide a roadmap for your side venture's success.

5. Test the market: Before fully committing to your side venture, test the market to validate your product or service. Offer samples or prototypes to potential customers, gather feedback, and assess their level of interest and willingness to pay. This will help you refine your offering and make necessary adjustments.

6. Build an online presence: Establish a professional online presence through a website or social media platforms relevant to your target audience. Showcase your products, services, or portfolio, and engage with potential customers through consistent and compelling content. Leverage social media marketing and SEO strategies to increase visibility and reach.

7. Price your offerings strategically: Determine your pricing structure based on factors such as production costs, market value, and perceived value. Consider your target audience's willingness to pay and competitor pricing. Experiment with different pricing models and strategies to find the optimal balance between profitability and customer satisfaction.

8. Develop effective marketing strategies: Utilize digital marketing techniques such as social media marketing, content marketing, email marketing, and influencer collaborations to promote your side venture. Build a strong brand identity and leverage storytelling to connect with your audience and convey the value of your offerings.

9. Provide excellent customer service: Focus on delivering exceptional customer service to build a loyal customer base and generate positive word-of-mouth referrals. Respond promptly to inquiries, address customer concerns, and aim for a seamless customer experience from start to finish.

10. Continuously learn and adapt: Stay updated on industry trends, customer preferences, and new opportunities within your chosen field. Seek feedback from customers, analyze your business performance, and be open to making necessary adjustments to improve your products, services, and processes.

Remember, turning your hobby into a profitable side venture may take time and effort. Stay committed, learn from your experiences, and remain passionate about what you're doing. With dedication and a customer-focused approach, you can create a successful and fulfilling business from your hobbies.

Managing multiple income streams and maximizing earnings potential

Managing multiple income streams and maximizing earnings potential requires careful planning and organization. Here are some strategies to help you effectively manage and optimize your various income streams:

1. Set clear goals and priorities: Define your financial goals and prioritize your income streams accordingly. Determine which streams are the most important to you and focus your energy and resources on maximizing their potential.

2. Diversify your income streams: Look for opportunities to diversify your income sources to reduce risk and increase potential earnings. Explore different avenues such as freelance work, investments, rental properties, online businesses, or passive income streams like royalties or affiliate marketing.

3. Efficient time management: Allocate your time effectively among your different income streams. Create a schedule or routine that allows you to dedicate focused time to each stream, ensuring that you're giving adequate attention to each one.

4. Streamline administrative tasks: Streamline and automate administrative tasks as much as possible. Use technology and tools to simplify bookkeeping, invoicing, tracking expenses, and managing customer or client communications. This will help you save time and focus on income-generating activities.

5. Leverage technology and systems: Utilize technology and systems to streamline your processes and optimize your income streams. This can include using project management tools, financial software, automation tools, and customer relationship management (CRM) systems to enhance productivity and efficiency.

6. Prioritize high-income activities: Identify the activities within each income stream that generate the highest returns and prioritize them. Focus on tasks and projects that have the potential to generate the most income or offer the best long-term prospects.

7. Continuously improve your skills and knowledge: Invest in your personal and professional development to enhance your earning potential. Stay updated on industry trends, acquire new skills, and seek opportunities for growth and advancement within each income stream.

8. Regularly review and adjust: Regularly assess the performance of your income streams. Analyze the revenue generated, identify areas for improvement, and make adjustments accordingly. This could involve refining your marketing strategies, increasing rates, expanding your product or service offerings, or cutting out low-performing ventures.

9. Maintain financial discipline: Practice sound financial management by budgeting, tracking expenses, and regularly reviewing your financial situation. Understand your cash flow, set aside savings, and reinvest in your income streams strategically.

10. Seek professional advice when needed: Consult with financial advisors, accountants, or business mentors who can provide guidance specific to your situation. They can help you optimize your income streams, minimize taxes, and offer valuable insights into wealth management.

Remember, managing multiple income streams requires dedication, discipline, and adaptability. Regularly assess your progress, stay open to new opportunities, and be willing to adjust your strategies to maximize your earnings potential over time.

Chapter 8

Digital Entrepreneurship

Strategies for Online Business Success

Identifying online business opportunities and niches

Identifying online business opportunities and niches involves finding areas where there is demand and room for growth in the digital space. Here are some steps to help you identify potential online business opportunities:

1. Identify your interests and expertise: Start by considering your passions, skills, and knowledge areas. Look for online business opportunities that align with your interests and where you can leverage your expertise.

2. Research market trends and demands: Stay updated on current market trends and identify emerging industries or areas experiencing growth. Look for gaps or underserved niches where you can offer unique products, services, or solutions.

3. Explore online communities and forums: Participate in online communities, forums, and social media groups related to your areas of interest. Engage in discussions, ask questions, and listen to the challenges and needs of the community members. This can provide valuable insights into potential business opportunities.

4. Conduct keyword research: Use keyword research tools to identify popular search terms and topics within your chosen industry. This can help you understand what people are searching for online and uncover potential niches with high demand and lower competition.

5. Analyze competitor landscapes: Study your competitors and analyze their strengths and weaknesses. Look for gaps or areas where you can differentiate yourself and offer unique value to customers. This could be through pricing, customer service, product innovation, or a different target audience.

6. Consider emerging technologies and platforms: Keep an eye on emerging technologies and platforms that are gaining traction. For example, the rise of virtual reality, blockchain, artificial intelligence, or voice assistants may create new opportunities for online businesses. Evaluate how you can leverage these technologies to create unique products or services.

7. Look for underserved or unmet needs: Identify pain points or needs that are not adequately addressed by existing solutions. Explore industries or customer segments where there is an opportunity to provide better experiences, convenience, or improved outcomes.

8. Test and validate your ideas: Once you have identified potential business opportunities, validate your ideas before fully committing. This can involve conducting surveys, running small-scale tests, or offering pilot versions of your products or services to gather feedback and assess market interest.

9. Understand the target audience: Gain a deep understanding of your target audience's demographics, interests, preferences, and purchasing behaviors. This will help you tailor your products, marketing messages, and customer experience to effectively reach and engage your target market.

10. Continuously adapt and innovate: Stay agile and adaptable in the online business space. Monitor industry trends, customer feedback, and market dynamics. Continuously seek opportunities for innovation, improvement, and expansion within your chosen niche.

Remember, choosing the right online business opportunity requires a combination of market research, understanding customer needs, and aligning with your own interests and expertise. It's essential to assess the feasibility and long-term sustainability of the opportunity before diving in. With thorough research and strategic planning, you can identify a profitable niche and establish a successful online business.

Building an online presence and leveraging digital marketing

Building an online presence and leveraging digital marketing strategies are essential for reaching and engaging with your target audience in the digital space. Here are some steps to help you build an effective online presence and leverage digital marketing:

1. Define your target audience: Clearly identify your target audience, including their demographics, interests, and online behaviors. This will help you tailor your online presence and marketing efforts to effectively reach and connect with them.

2. Build a professional website: Create a user-friendly and visually appealing website that represents your brand. Ensure it provides relevant information about your products or services, showcases your expertise, and includes clear calls-to-action for visitors to engage with your business.

3. Optimize your website for search engines (SEO): Implement search engine optimization (SEO) strategies to improve your website's visibility in search engine results. This involves using relevant keywords, creating quality content, optimizing meta tags, and building backlinks from reputable sources.

4. Establish a content marketing strategy: Develop a content marketing strategy to provide value to your target audience and build brand credibility. Create and distribute relevant and engaging content such as blog posts, articles, videos, podcasts, or infographics. Share your content on your website, social media platforms, and through email marketing.

5. Leverage social media platforms: Identify the social media platforms where your target audience is most active and establish a presence on those channels. Share engaging content, interact with your audience, and use social media advertising to reach a wider audience and promote your products or services.

6. Engage in influencer marketing: Collaborate with influencers or industry experts who have a significant following and influence in your target market. Partnering with influencers can help expand your reach, build brand awareness, and generate trust among their followers.

7. Utilize email marketing: Build an email list of interested prospects and customers and leverage email marketing campaigns to nurture relationships, share valuable content, promote offers, and drive conversions. Personalize your emails and segment your audience to deliver targeted and relevant messages.

8. Embrace video marketing: Incorporate video content into your digital marketing strategy. Create informative and engaging videos that showcase your products or services, provide tutorials or demonstrations, share customer testimonials, or deliver industry insights. Utilize platforms like YouTube, Vimeo, or social media to share and promote your videos.

9. Monitor and analyze data: Use web analytics tools to track and measure the performance of your online presence and digital marketing efforts. Analyze data such as website traffic, engagement metrics, conversion rates, and customer behavior to gain insights and optimize your strategies.

10. Stay up-to-date with industry trends: Continuously stay informed about changes and trends in the digital marketing landscape. Attend webinars, conferences, and industry events, and follow reputable sources and thought leaders in the digital marketing space. Adapt your strategies to leverage emerging technologies and new opportunities.

Remember, building a strong online presence and leveraging digital marketing is an ongoing process. Consistency, relevance, and continuous improvement are key. Regularly evaluate and adjust your strategies based on data and customer feedback to optimize your online presence and drive meaningful results for your business.

Scaling and optimizing your digital business for long-term success

Scaling and optimizing your digital business is crucial for long-term success and growth. Here are some strategies to help you scale and optimize your digital business:

1. Set clear goals and develop a growth strategy: Define your long-term goals and develop a strategic plan to achieve them. Identify the key metrics you'll use to measure success and outline the steps required to scale your business.

2. Automate processes and workflows: Implement automation tools and systems to streamline repetitive tasks and improve operational efficiency. This can include automating email marketing, customer support, inventory management, and analytics reporting.

3. Focus on customer experience: Prioritize delivering an exceptional customer experience at every touchpoint. Invest in user-friendly website design, provide personalized support, and continuously seek customer feedback to improve your products, services, and overall experience.

4. Optimize conversion rates: Continuously analyze and optimize your conversion funnels to maximize the number of visitors who convert into customers. Implement A/B testing, improve website navigation, simplify checkout processes, and utilize persuasive copy and calls-to-action to increase conversions.

5. Implement a data-driven approach: Collect and analyze data to gain insights into customer behavior, market trends, and the performance of your digital business. Use tools like Google Analytics, heat maps, and customer surveys to make informed decisions and optimize your strategies.

6. Expand your marketing efforts: Diversify and expand your digital marketing efforts to reach a wider audience. Explore additional channels such as influencer partnerships, affiliate marketing, content syndication, or targeted online advertising to increase brand visibility and attract new customers.

7. Foster customer loyalty and retention: Implement strategies to retain existing customers and encourage repeat purchases. This can include loyalty programs, personalized offers, email marketing campaigns, and proactive customer support. Happy and loyal customers can become brand advocates and contribute to your business growth through word-of-mouth.

8. Continuously innovate and adapt: Stay agile and embrace innovation in your digital business. Keep an eye on emerging technologies, industry trends, and changing customer needs.

Be open to new ideas, test and iterate on new features or offerings, and continuously seek ways to improve and stay ahead of the competition.

9. Build strategic partnerships: Explore strategic partnerships and collaborations with complementary businesses or influencers in your industry. Partnering with others can help expand your reach, access new markets, share resources, and leverage each other's strengths.

10. Invest in talent and resources: As your business scales, invest in the right talent and resources to support your growth. This may include hiring skilled employees or outsourcing certain tasks to experts in areas like marketing, operations, or customer service.

Remember, scaling and optimizing a digital business is an ongoing process. Continuously monitor your progress, measure results, and adapt your strategies based on data and market feedback. Stay proactive, customer-centric, and innovative to ensure long-term success in the digital space.

Conclusion

Embracing Financial Empowerment in the Digital Age

Embracing financial empowerment in the digital age involves leveraging digital tools, resources, and knowledge to take control of your financial well-being. Here are some ways to embrace financial empowerment in the digital age:

1. Educate yourself: Take advantage of the abundance of online resources, courses, and educational platforms available to enhance your financial literacy. Educate yourself on topics such as budgeting, saving, investing, debt management, and retirement planning. Understanding these concepts will empower you to make informed financial decisions.

2. Utilize personal finance apps and tools: Embrace the power of personal finance apps and digital tools that can help you track your expenses, create budgets, and manage your financial goals. These tools often provide real-time insights into your spending habits, automate savings, and provide personalized recommendations to optimize your finances.

3. Automate savings and investments: Take advantage of digital automation to make saving and investing a seamless process. Set up automatic transfers from your checking account to a dedicated savings or investment account. Consider investing in low-cost index funds or utilizing robo-advisors for automated investment management.

4. Track and manage your credit: Use online tools and credit monitoring services to keep track of your credit score and credit report. Regularly review your credit report for errors and take steps to improve your credit score. Digital platforms can also help you manage your credit card usage, track rewards, and find the best credit card options for your needs.

5. Explore digital banking services: Embrace the convenience of digital banking services that offer features such as online banking, mobile banking apps, digital wallets, and remote deposit. These services allow you to manage your finances, make transactions, and access your accounts anytime, anywhere.

6. Protect your online identity and financial information: With the increased digitization of financial transactions, it's crucial to prioritize online security. Safeguard your personal and financial information by using strong passwords, enabling two-factor authentication, and being cautious of phishing attempts. Regularly monitor your financial accounts for any unauthorized activity.

7. Embrace online investing platforms: Consider utilizing online investing platforms that provide easy access to a range of investment options. Many online brokerages offer low fees, user-friendly interfaces, and educational resources to help you make informed investment decisions.

8. Explore alternative financial services: Investigate innovative financial services offered by fintech companies, such as peer-to-peer lending, crowdfunding, or digital wallets for cryptocurrencies. These services can provide alternative opportunities for borrowing, investing, or managing your money.

9. Seek financial advice online: Use online resources, financial blogs, and communities to gain insights and advice from financial experts. Engage in online forums or social media groups focused on personal finance to exchange ideas, ask questions, and learn from others' experiences.

10. Stay informed and adapt to change: The digital landscape is continuously evolving, so it's important to stay informed about new financial technologies, regulations, and market trends. Be open to adapting your financial strategies as new

opportunities arise or as your goals and
circumstances change.

By embracing financial empowerment in the
digital age, you can leverage technology and
digital resources to gain control over your
finances, make informed decisions, and work
toward your financial goals with confidence.